PLAN YOUR ESTATE THE RIGHT WAY!

Useful Information That Will Protect Your Family's Future In California

Benjamin Diederich, Esq.

Jacobs & Whitehall
73-03 Bell Blvd, #10
Oakland Gardens, NY 11364
www.jacobsandwhitehall.com

Ordering Information:
Quantity sales. Special discounts are available on quantity purchases by corporations, associations, and others. For details, contact the publisher at the address above.
Orders by U.S. trade bookstores and wholesalers. Please contact Jacobs & Whitehall: Tel: (888) 991-2766 or visit www.jacobsandwhitehall.com.
Printed in the United States of America
Published in 2021

ISBN: 978-1-951149-38-3

PREFACE

As someone who has lost a parent too young, I have made it my mission to ensure that no one leaves their family unprepared for the future and at a loss of how to move forward.

Whether that means ensuring that their family is not forced into court and conflict for months upon months during the most difficult time of having recently lost a parent.

Whether that means ensuring financial assets are passed on in a secure manner that won't end up squandered by children not yet ready for them.

Whether that means ensuring that your voice, your stories, your wisdom – not just your financial assets – are secured and passed on to your children and your future generations.

In any case, we strive to be there for you and your family.

Dedication

To Jennifer, my partner in life who supports me in every endeavor and drives me to do more, be more, and be better. I wouldn't want to do any of this without you, my love.

To Cameron, the sweetest, smartest, funniest, hardest working little girl I've ever known. You will always be my little angel. I love you to the moon and back, to infinity and beyond, and farther than Captain Marvel can fly.

DISCLAIMER

This publication is intended to be used for educational purposes only. No legal advice is being given, and no attorney-client relationship is intended to be created by reading this material. The author assumes no liability for any errors or omissions or for how this book or its contents are used or interpreted, or for any consequences resulting directly or indirectly from the use of this book. For legal or any other advice, please consult an experienced attorney or the appropriate expert, who is aware of the specific facts of your case and is knowledgeable in the law in your jurisdiction.

Law Office of Benjamin Diederich
29826 Haun Road #311
Menifee, CA 92586
(951) 332-7079
www.protectorlaw.com

TESTIMONIALS

"Ben was awesome with my senior parents. He made things simple and absolutely complete for us. He eased all of our anxieties and did beautiful work even working with my brother from another state. I took all of the Trust work to my parents new bank in another state today and the banker immediately said she LOVES our attorney because it's was so well done she didn't have to dig for ANYTHING. She's been doing this for years and she had never seen anything like it. Truly! Ben was an answer to our prayers at this challenging time in my parents' life. I cannot speak highly enough of Ben and Nicole. Please, please, please do not look further if you are looking for an attorney to help your family. Ben, thank you for what you did for my family."

– Peggy C.

****

"Ben did a fantastic job setting up our Trust. We knew the importance of setting up a living trust but found out there is a difference between doing it right and just doing it. He patiently explained everything as we worked through the details. When we were done, it felt like a weight had been lifted from our shoulders. Nicole truly is a "go-to" resource for us, answering what seemed to be an endless stream of questions. We are so grateful we found LOBD! Words can't express our appreciation."

– Bill & Eileen

****

"My husband and I met Ben Diederich at a living trust workshop. He was very pleasant, easy to talk with, and knows what he's talking about. He gave valuable information never trying to sell us on anything. We are so happy with how he cared for us. He's a man of integrity and his word. Honestly, we had heard setting up a living trust was a pain but our experience was nothing like that. We had a great time talking and joking with Ben and his assistant Nicole (what a sweet women). We would not hesitate to recommend Ben. We even invited Ben and Nicole for thanksgiving dinner."

– Traci A.

****

"I have known Ben for several years and worked with him on various occasions. Ben is extremely knowledgeable, trustworthy, and efficient, and he has achieved great results for me. He is a great attorney, and I wouldn't go to anyone else with issues regarding intellectual property. In fact, I generally consult with Ben on any legal issues I encounter and always highly value his thoughts and advice."

– General Counsel

****

"We were very happy with how you helped our parents. They were pleased as well, of course! We very much appreciated how you fielded our remotely-asked questions as well as the in-person interactions. Thank you so much for your patience, your care, your guidance, expertise and your dedication to conscientious practice. God bless you all!"

– Patrick

****

"From the time you walk in (there's a welcome sign with your names on it) until you leave with paperwork in hand, Nicole & Ben go out of their way to make you comfortable and give you the best experience possible. Even after your business is completed they find ways to make you smile. So glad we found them to take care of our Living Trust & will."

- Mike

****

"We had such a great experience with Ben and his office. Everything was explained clearly and up front. The timeline in getting our will and estate planning done was realistic and understandable. Ben and his office is down to earth, friendly, patient, kind, and professional. We have already recommended him to others who need an attorney."

- Thomas W.

****

"Ben is very knowledgeable in the areas of law he practices. I've known him for some time now and find that he's not only meticulous but has a great personal touch. I would be happy to recommend him to my closest friends."

- Manager

****

"Ben and Nichole were efficient and patient with my situation and even though I probably didn't need their services at this time I felt that if I did they were going to have my back moving forward. Thanks again."

- Rick

****

"Very professional yet friendly and pleasant. Efficient and helpful. A task that could have been stressful and overwhelming was easygoing and manageable."

– Becky H.

****

"Great service, very knowledgeable and patient with all my questions. I would highly recommend him!"

– Iris

****

"Ben and Nicole, you treated us with the utmost caring and respect in helping us to establish our Trust. We cannot thank you enough."

– Wayne C.

****

TABLE OF CONTENTS

i. Preface iii

ii. Dedication iv

iii. Disclaimer v

iv. Testimonials vi

v. About The Author 1

1. What Is Estate Planning? 4

2. Will And Its Functions 7

3. Trust, Its Benefits And Limitations 10

4. Things To Consider When Planning Your Estate For Children 13

5. Guardianship And Its Meaning 15

6. Probate And Common Misconceptions 21

7. Common Misunderstandings About Estate Planning 25

8. Pitfalls Of Planning Your Estate Without An Attorney 29

vi. Index 32

vii. Notes 34

About The Author

I am Ben Diederich, owner of the Law Office of Benjamin Diederich. I started my legal career at an intellectual property boutique law firm, as a registered patent attorney. When my wife and I moved back to our suburban hometown in 2016, I decided to open my firm and no longer commute. Our firm handles intellectual property matters, including patents, trademarks, and copyrights. While we still love working with our intellectual property clients all around the country, when I opened my firm I wanted to have a practice area where I could work with the local community and help support it.

Specifically, I've gone through the loss of a parent, grandparents, and other family members, and I've seen what it looks like when you've done planning and what it looks like when you haven't done planning. I wanted to help families avoid some of the issues that happen if you don't do the planning, so I started to focus on estate planning in our practice and have never looked back. We love getting to know each family's story, and help them move forward in a way where the know their family will avoid court and conflict when something does happen to them.

What Is The Purpose Of Writing This Book?

I want my readers to not be scared of the estate planning process but to also not put it off for another day. One of the main target audiences that we work with are families with minor children. We want to make sure that those children would be completely taken care of if something were to happen to their parents.

Who Is This Book For?

This book is for anyone who owns a home, has kids, or owns their own business. In California, if you own a home, your family is probably going to end up going through probate if you haven't done proper estate planning.

CHAPTER 1

WHAT IS ESTATE PLANNING?

Estate planning is about what you want to achieve for your family. That is where the benefits of working with an attorney come in, versus doing it yourself. It is thinking about the things you might not realize could happen. It is more than just a will; you want to have your healthcare directives taken care of and have powers of attorney in place.

The Goal Of Estate Planning

The goal of estate planning should be to help keep your family out of conflict and out of court. It should be making your family's life easier, now that you're no longer there. The worst thing is to lose a family member and spend the next 18 months in probate court, in a public setting, and relive all of this before you can move on.

Key Life Events That Are Considered During Estate Planning

One of the biggest events is when people come in and out of your life. When you're doing your estate planning, you're going to be naming the people who are going to run your finances for you, after you're gone. You'll also be naming the people who are going to be receiving your assets. You want to make sure that the people you named continue to be the ones you would choose for these positions. If you get divorced, you want to make sure that your ex is not still making your medical and financial decisions just because you didn't take them off of your estate plan.

Best Ways To Protect My Legacy For My Children Or Other Heirs

The key is having a well-thought and written succession plan. You need to figure out if you're a business owner and something happens to you, who is going to come in and keep that business going. Another thing you need to think about is how that is going to be funded. These matters can be handled by different types of buy-sell agreements or life insurance policies so that the business can continue and your beneficiaries still receive the benefits.

How Often Do We Need To Review Or Update Our Estate Planning Documents?

Any time something in your life changes, you should update your documents. Any time the applicable laws change, you should update your documents. We bring everyone back in at least every three years. Some people need more than that but we try to catch changes and update the plans before something happens.

CHAPTER 2

WILL AND ITS FUNCTIONS

A will is a document that is intended to be used by the court, through the probate process, to let them know how you want your assets to be distributed. If you have minor children, it will also name who you want the guardians of your children to be. Many people think that drafting a will can avoid probate but in reality, having only a will guarantees that your family will end up in probate.

A will becomes effective once you pass away. If you become incapacitated, your will doesn't go into effect. There can be times where family members aren't able to make decisions because you haven't passed, so you want to have powers of attorney in place for while you're incapacitated.

Will As A Part Of Estate Planning Documents

Everyone who does estate planning is going to have a will. If they don't need a trust, they will have a will to say what happens to their assets after they're gone. If you do create a trust, you're still going to have a will. In that case, it is a more simplified version of a will, called a pour-over will. The whole reason for the existence of that pour-over will is in case you don't fully fund your trust. If you pass away and something didn't get transferred over into the trust, and it's still in your name, you're instructing the court to put it into the trust and disperse it per the terms of the trust.

Limitations To A Will

The biggest limitation with a will is that it is going to guarantee that you end up in probate court if you just have the will on its own. There is also future planning that you can do for your children to leave your assets to them in a protected fashion, which you can't do with a will. It needs to be by the way of a trust. Sometimes, a will can be enough. If your assets are limited and you don't have anything that would put you into probate court, a will is sufficient. However, you still need additional documents in your estate plan, such as advanced healthcare directives and financial powers of attorney.

CHAPTER 3

TRUST, ITS BENEFITS AND LIMITATIONS

A trust is an agreement between three parties: the trust maker, the trustee, who oversees and runs the trust, and the beneficiaries. Beneficiaries are third parties who are going to benefit from the trust. What we deal with most is called a revocable living trust. In revocable living trusts, you are the trust maker, the trustee, and the beneficiary, while you're alive. You can still sell, buy, and move your assets in and out of the trust. You're not limited in any way, while you're still alive.

One of the largest benefits of the trust is that since your assets are held in the name of the trust rather than your name individually, you don't have to go through the probate process after you die. Another huge benefit is that they can be effective even while you're incapacitated. With a trust, you can have strong incapacitation provisions that allow someone to step in and manage things for you while you're incapacitated. If you regain your capacity, you can regain control.

Limitations To A Trust

The biggest limitation to a trust is that there is some extra expense in creating it and transferring your assets into it. If you don't move your assets into the trust, it does no good. You just wasted your money and your family is going to end up in probate.

Common Types Of Trusts And Their Purposes

There is a revocable living trust, which is a simple trust that you set up for the benefit of yourself while you're alive. It is revocable, so you can amend it at any time, and you are not limited. There are also irrevocable living trusts and those are for more complicated situations, such as people with extremely large estates that need to do tax planning and those who have a child receiving benefits from the government. An irrevocable living trust is very specialized and rare, in comparison to a revocable living trust.

CHAPTER 4

THINGS TO CONSIDER WHEN PLANNING YOUR ESTATE FOR CHILDREN

If you are gone, who is going to take care of your children? How are they, financially, going to be taken care of? Should you be choosing guardians that have enough money to take care of your kids or is that something that shouldn't be a consideration? Should you have enough life insurance policies so that you can pick the person who would raise your kids the way you would want them to be raised?

If the people that you want to be your long-term guardians live in another state and it is going to take time for them to be notified and to get there, what should the police do in the meantime? You want to make sure that you have temporary guardians in mind, who can take your children until the long-term guardians can come and get them. You also want to think about passing on certain things to your children, such as the life stories, experience, and wisdom that you would have wanted to share with them.

CHAPTER 5

GUARDIANSHIP AND ITS MEANING

Guardians are people you name to take care of your minor children if you are no longer able to do so. Very few people have picked guardians for their children if something were to happen to them. If you don't choose who your guardians are going to be for your children, someone has to choose for you. A judge is going to make that decision, based on the information they have available. However, they might not know everything. They might not make the same choice you would have.

Is Naming A Guardian Enough?

There are lots of issues when you think about who you're going to name as a guardian. If you pick a married couple to be the guardians of your children, do you want it to be those people only if they remain married? If they were to split up, which one would you want to remain the guardian of your children? What if something happens to the person you named and now you have no one named? You want to have backup guardians named, in case the first-place people are not able to serve.

Do I Need To Consider Excluding Possible Guardians That I Had Never Thought Of?

We focus a lot on working with parents of minor children and we have very detailed documents regarding the children that go above and beyond what most estate planning attorneys cover. One of those aspects that we look at is whether you need to confidentially exclude potential guardians. You may have multiple siblings and you don't want them to be fighting over who is going to be getting your children.

Sometimes, one sibling might look like a great guardian on paper. They might be very successful, have a good job, and have a nice home. Another sibling isn't so successful and is not as financially secure, but you know that the more successful sibling has an issue that isn't public. You don't want that person raising your children. The judge might never know that private information and might choose that sibling to be the guardian of your children. If you have someone in your life that might potentially step up to be the guardian and you know they should not be raising your children, you need to plan ahead and confidentially exclude those people from being in the running.

How Can I Pass On More Than Just My Financial Wealth To My Children?

Another thing that is somewhat unique to our practice is passing on not just financial assets, but wisdom, experiences, or stories to your children. We use a three-meeting plan system and on that third meeting, we do what we call family legacy recordings. We record a series of questions and you get an audio recording of you sharing your wisdom, stories, and memories with your children so that in the future, they can revisit you. When people come back over the years, we'll record further conversations and they can create a library of recordings for their family.

How To Determine Who To Appoint As A Standby And A Permanent Guardian?

For the standby temporary guardian, you want someone you know and trust, who is local and can get to your house within about 30 minutes. This way, your children never have to go into the custody of the state while waiting for the long term guardians to come. For long-term guardians, you want to pick people you think would raise your children similar to the way that you would want them to be raised. Financial considerations should never be an issue; you should never avoid picking someone to be your guardian because they don't have enough money.

As a parent, you must ensure that your children are taken care of, and that includes financial security. You should have life insurance policies in place if you don't have the assets together so that financial concerns are never an issue when you're nominating your guardians. As part of our planning for children, we prepare detailed instructions for guardians to give them information on how you would want your children to be raised.

What Decisions Can Be Made For My Child Or Children By A Guardian?

A long-term guardian takes on the role of the parent, so they can make the same decisions that you would make. Once approved by the court, they are the new parents of your children and can make every decision.

What Happens If You Don't Include Provisions For A Guardian?

If you have not named a guardian, the court has no choice but to have the judge decide who should be the guardians for your children. Hopefully, you have family members who are going to step up and say that they want to raise your children. The bigger issue can be when you have multiple people step up and say they are the ones who should become the guardians of your children. Then, you can have years of contention and fighting in court to figure out who is going to be the ultimate guardian of these children.

Protecting The Assets That You Leave To Your Children Well Into The Future

Another thing you can do with trust-based planning is leave your financial assets to your children in a protected fashion. Most people would like to own their assets in a way that couldn't be taken away by a lawsuit or creditors. It is very difficult to protect our assets that way in California. However, with trust-based planning, you can leave assets to your children in an ongoing trust, also called a lifetime asset protection trust, so that these assets are passed to your children in a protected fashion. If they were to get sued, those assets wouldn't be touchable. If they were to get divorced, they wouldn't lose half of those assets in the divorce. If they had credit issues, the creditors wouldn't be able to touch those assets. It is a great gift for your children to leave them these assets in a protected fashion. It gives them the incentive to leave the money in the trust and create something out of it.

CHAPTER 6

PROBATE AND COMMON MISCONCEPTIONS

Probate is a lawsuit filed against you for the benefit of your creditors. It is a fully public court proceeding that takes, in California, about 12 to 18 months to get through. There is an open record for everyone to see an accounting of your assets and your debts. Your creditors come in and claim your estate to get paid. Whatever is leftover gets dispersed to your beneficiaries and your heirs. There are a lot of things that are troublesome or difficult with probate. It takes a long time and it is expensive, between the court fees, attorney's fees, assessment fees, and bonds that might have to be posted.

The costs are estimated to be about five percent of the gross value of your estate. It is very easy, in California, to have a million-dollar estate, between the value of a house (not the equity, but the fair market value), bank accounts, and investments, which would cost your family roughly $50,000 to go through the probate process. Another downside of probate is that it is fully public. People scour these probate records and will see that a young person is coming into a large amount of money. They will then prey on them through scams. Even though estate planning may cost you some upfront, the amount that you are saving for your family by avoiding probate is huge.

Assets Subject To Probate

Anyone in California who has assets titled in their name above $166,250 (tied to inflation) is subject to probate, if they haven't done further planning.

Again, this is the fair market value of the assets, what they would be sold for, not necessarily the equity you may or may not have in them. Certain assets don't count towards your probate estate. If you have life insurance policies and you're designating beneficiaries, those pass outside of probate. Retirement accounts, 401ks, and IRAs, where you've named beneficiaries, are not subject to probate either. While life insurance and retirement accounts are not normally subject to probate, many people name their minor children as contingent beneficiaries, which results in these assets now having to go through the probate process!

Matters Of Concern Vis-à-vis Probate And How To Avoid Them

The biggest matters of concern regarding probate are that it is time-consuming, expensive, completely public, and it is for the benefit of your creditors, not for the benefit of you or your family. The best way to avoid probate is to create a fully funded revocable living trust. By fully funded, I mean you have the trust in place and you retitle your assets into the name of the trust. There is no point in creating a trust if you're not going to fund the trust. Another important thing is proper beneficiary designations which will help you avoid probate, such as not naming minor children on life insurance policies and retirement accounts. Owning your home as a joint tenancy with an adult child can also help keep you out of probate but can raise all kinds of other issues that would probably be better served by putting it into a trust instead.

CHAPTER 7

COMMON MISUNDERSTANDINGS ABOUT ESTATE PLANNING

The most common misunderstanding about estate planning is that people think they're too young to create an estate plan. They think this is something that only old people need to do, or that they don't have enough assets to even bother going through the process. Secondly, people put together a will through online websites or a relative who is a lawyer and think that is sufficient for their family to be taken care of.

Many people also believe that a trust they created decades ago is still all they need. That is far from the truth. As time goes on, the laws change, the people in your lives change, and what you own changes. It is not a one-and-done event. It is something that should be reviewed periodically to make sure that it still makes sense for you and your family.

People think estate planning is either for wealthy people or it is an estate sale, selling off the property after someone dies. It is really difficult to impress upon people that it is for everyone and that everyone needs to do some planning for their family's future. In California, for years, the minimum amount you needed to own that would put you into probate was $150,000 worth of total assets. In 2020, it went up to $166,250 (with future increases for inflation). People don't realize that this limit is on the gross value of their assets. If your home is worth more than $166,000, even if you have no equity in it, it would end up going through probate. In California, there is almost no such thing as a home worth less than $166,000.

Is It Ever Too Late To Start Planning For Your Assets And Loved Ones?

The ideal time to start planning is probably yesterday. The next most ideal time would be now. If you have anything you want to leave to people that need to be taken care of, now would be the time to do it. If you're married, have kids, or own a home, now is the time to start planning.

Is It A Onetime Planning Document For Estate Planning Or Is It More Than That?

A lot of attorneys provide one-off transactions. They tell clients to call them if something changes in the future. It is never looked at again by most people. A good portion of our practice involves reviewing trusts that have been drafted by other attorneys in the past. People will come in with their trust that was created 20 years ago. Many times, the trustee or successor trustee is someone who is no longer in their life. It is something that should be looked at periodically, unless you have a very simple life with very simple assets, and nothing ever changes. Even then, the laws change periodically. We bring people back in, free of charge, every three years, to review their plans. Some people need more updating than that, so we have plans where people come in every year to see what might need to be addressed.

CHAPTER 8

PITFALLS OF PLANNING YOUR ESTATE WITHOUT AN ATTORNEY

If you're going to go to an online website or software program for estate planning, it doesn't provide you any meaningful guidance. If you know what all the options mean and what the ramifications of making those choices are going to be, then that is great. The vast majority of people, even attorneys who aren't estate planners, don't realize what all of those ramifications are. There are too many things that they don't think about, like naming temporary guardians. They don't think about whether they need to exclude people as potential guardians or protect assets. If you know what you're doing, you can do it yourself. However, most people don't realize the ramifications of something so complicated, and you never know what you don't know.

Major Pitfalls That Can Come From Creating Your Own Estate Plan

The biggest pitfall is creating trusts and not funding them. We see people come in who have created a trust but didn't realize the importance of funding it. Working with an attorney who doesn't think about this issue is not helping you either. Oftentimes, people only have one person named in each role. The problem is, something can happen to that person before your plan goes into effect and you haven't named anyone else.

What Sets You And Your Firm Apart In Handling Estate Planning Matters?

I think what matters is being comfortable with the person you're working with and getting the guidance you need, not just getting a standardized form. It's about really customizing a plan for you, your family, and your family's needs. Some of the things that we do go above and beyond what most other attorneys do, in this field. That includes the three-meeting process, where we bring you back in and make sure that your assets are being funded into your trust. I don't want you to spend money on me creating this trust for you and then it never gets funded, and your family ends up in probate court anyway.

We also pass on more than just the financial assets with the family legacy conversations that we do, where we share your memories, experiences, and wisdom. We also bring everyone back regularly, either every three years or every year, and make sure that their plan is still working for them.

INDEX

B

Beneficiaries · 21
buy-sell agreements · 17

C

creditors · 31

E

estate planning · 36

F

family legacy recordings · 28

G

Guardians · 26

I

irrevocable living trusts · 22

J

joint tenancy · 35

L

life insurance policies · 17
long-term guardians · 25

M

minor children · 18

P

pour-over will · 19
Probate · 32
probate court · 16
public court proceeding · 32

R

revocable living trusts · 21

S

successor trustee · 38

T

tax planning · 23
temporary guardians · 25
three-meeting plan system · 28
trust · 21
trust-based planning · 31
trustee · 38

W

will · 18

NOTES

Made in the USA
Monee, IL
14 November 2026

68086551R00029